SOMETIMES I'M AFRAID

A BOOK ABOUT FEAR

Written by

Michaelene Mundy

Illustrated by

Ani  itzGerald

ABBEY PRESS Publications

1 Hill Drive

St. Meinrad, IN 47577

Text © 2012 Michaelene Mundy
Illustrations © 2012 St. Meinrad Archabbey
Published by Abbey Press Publications
1 Hill Drive
St. Meinrad, Indiana 47577

Library of Congress Catalog Number
2012905278

ISBN 978-0-87029-500-3

Printed in the United States of America.

A Message from the Author
to Parents and Caring Adults

We want our kids to be safe, happy, and well-adjusted. But we all know that our children, like us, have to face a lot of difficult things in their lives. And one of them is fear.

Most fears that children face are normal things like fear of the dark, anxiety about illness—their own or a family member's family conflicts, doing well in school, not making friends. Most of these things get worked out in the day-to-day activities and adventures of life. We hope that this book can make these fears clearer and maybe easier to understand for a child and even for us adults. We also hope that this book will give the child some coping skills as well as a better perspective. Sometimes a bit of humor can even be helpful.

We adults have learned that one of the best overall remedies for tackling fears (and practically everything else) is an abundance of love and care…along with some common sense, patience, and the commitment to really "be there" for a child.

—*Michaelene Mundy*

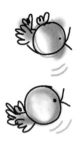

What does "Afraid" feel like?

You've been afraid, so you already know what it feels like!

It can be a cold and chilly feeling, or a shaking, quaking feeling all over.

It's a funny feeling in your stomach— maybe even a stomachache.

It is mainly a bad feeling and one that you feel like you can't make better. But there are ways to make things better.

It's good to be afraid of some things.

Everyone is afraid of something. And that's good. Being afraid of fire, or afraid to run out into the street, being afraid of strangers, or to hit a great big bully is a good thing.

Being careful is important. If you were never afraid, you might do things that could hurt you or put you in danger.

Being afraid can also be a problem.

If you are afraid of too many things, though, it can be a problem. It can keep you from learning, from sleeping, from having fun.

You might not discover a fun ride at the amusement park or that the cold water in the swimming pool feels warmer after a while.

Being afraid can even get us into trouble.

If you accidentally break something, your dad or mom might ask, "Who broke that?" You might be afraid to say that you broke it because you don't want anyone to be mad at you.

If you don't say anything, or tell a lie, you might get someone else in trouble. That doesn't feel good either.

Be brave. It's always better to tell the truth, and that takes courage.

Courage is what we need.

Having courage means we do things that are right even when we are afraid.

This might mean raising your hand in class even if you are not sure you have the right answer.

It might mean being nice to someone no one else seems to like.

What can we do when we're afraid?

Lots of times it helps to talk with Mom or Dad, an adult friend, or a teacher about something you are afraid of. They can often help you. They will understand.

People older than you have been and are still afraid of some things, too—like sharks, or getting lost going to a new place.

Maybe a better way.

Something that you can do for real is just to quiet down—breathe very S L O W L Y in and out, in and out. This can help the scared feeling a lot.

A lot of grown-ups do this before they give a speech, or before they start a new job.

Even better ways to handle being afraid.

Learning about the things you are afraid of can help. It's called "getting the facts."

If you are afraid a monster is living under your bed, you can read about other children who were afraid of this and how they handled it.

Sometimes these stories will make you laugh and feel better.

Are you afraid of the dark?

At night when things get quiet, you may sometimes hear noises and wonder what they are. Or maybe you think you can see things that aren't really there. Your sleepy mind can trick you.

Maybe a night-light in your room can help chase away shadows and let you see everything is all right. The sounds may be coming from the street outside your house or from your sister's video game.

Thinking happy thoughts can help.

Maybe you can't sleep because you are afraid of something that might happen at school tomorrow or at the doctor's office. It helps to think happy thoughts. The teacher or the doctor want to help you, not hurt you.

Yes, it hurts a little to get a shot, and it hurts inside when the teacher asks you and you don't know the answer to a question. But things like these help us stay healthy and keep learning things.

Thinking of God's love and care helps, too.

The Bible is full of stories that tell us not to be afraid. It does not say that some bad things will not happen. But it does say that God's love—and the love from our family and neighbors and friends…and even strangers—will help us no matter what might happen.

Being afraid of strangers.

Your parents may tell you not to talk to strangers, if you are not with a grown-up.

Everyone is a stranger the first time we meet them—your teacher was a stranger on the first day of school.

We always want to try to be safe, but if we were afraid of everyone we do not know, it would be a very scary world.

Afraid of making mistakes?

We all want to do what is right. Everyone wishes they knew all the answers in a test or at school. We all wish we could speak and act perfectly. All of your life you will learn more and more things you did not know before.

Making mistakes, and being afraid of "failing" at something, is normal. It means you want to learn and then you work harder and remember things for the next time.

You can help someone else who is afraid!

If you notice a friend is afraid of something, or if someone tells you they are afraid, maybe you can help. You can do this by listening to them, by telling them what you did when YOU were afraid. You can also help them by just being their friend.

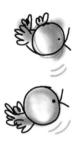

Michaelene Mundy has written a number of books for children. She is a school and community counselor and author of *Sad Isn't Bad* and *Mad Isn't Bad*, both a part of the Abbey Press series of Elf-help Books for Kids. She has taught elementary school children and with her husband, Linus, wrote the *Bringing Religion Home* newsletter for a number of years.

Anne FitzGerald is an internationally known artist and has written and illustrated over 200 children's books. She is creator of "Dear God Kids" and many other children's books and products. Anne works from her studio/gallery in Limerick, Ireland, and teaches art in Liberty Christian School there.